and I close my eyes

HAILEY MARIE

And I Close My Eyes
Copyright © 2021 by Hailey Burns

Any people referenced in this collection may be representations of thoughts, struggles, or emotions, and some may represent real people. No identifying information in any form is given and it is up to readers to determine if the referenced person is a concept or a living being.

All rights reserved. No part of this book may be reproduced or used in any manner without written permission of the copyright owner except for the use of quotations in a book review. For more information, address:

First paperback edition: April 2021

Edited by Galli Huaute
Cover and interior design by Natalia Junqueira

ISBN 978-1-7366-5730-0 (paperback)
ISBN 978-1-7366-5731-7 (ebook)

www.hailmarie.com
Twitter: @HMariePoetry
Instagram: @HaileyMariePoetry
haileymariepoetry@gmail.com

Author's Note

This poetry collection is a peek into the healing process I went through to overcome past trauma, mental health issues, and the disasters of everyday life including heartbreak and stress. These poems range from being very dark to being very positive and hopeful because that is how healing works. Although my collection progresses in a straightforward line, my healing was not like that. Progress and healing is a very curvy path that includes steps forward and steps backward over and over again before you make it to the end. I stress this here and in my final thoughts because that is a difficult lesson to learn, one that I did not learn on my own. I arranged this collection this way so that hope was easy to find when you needed it, and so poems about fighting or fear and despair were easy to find when you needed to feel heard and less alone, because we all need that sometimes - even when it hurts. Although this collection makes it seem like my journey is over, it's not. Mentally healing and overcoming mental health issues is very difficult and it takes much time and patience. It is a battle that will start back up every now and then when it feels the need to. I overcame the most difficult part, which was finding my footing and getting on the right path. I took the steps to get help and participated in working toward my hope, and in the end, it was all worth it. I have many more good days than bad days, and every time I work past a period of struggles, it gets easier when they stop by again. It gets easier every time I prove to myself that I can do it. My journey may never be over, but the hard part is, and if you are in the depths of the most difficult times in your battle, keep fighting. You will make it through and each time it will get easier. Keep fighting even when you are tired, even when you feel like you can't take it anymore because there will be better days. You can reach your hopes.

I struggled a bit with deciding on how to illustrate the poems in this collection because clean illustrations are more professional and well… clean, but that is not what these poems are about. In the end, the only thing that felt right was to create messy, sketch-like, imperfect, and unfinished drawings because we are unfinished people. We will always be unfinished. Every line is a piece of who we are and we are messy, certainly not clean and precise. We are humans; we learn and grow. A single stray mark does not define us, the picture as a whole is who we are. Each line is just a step on the way to being whole. I wanted this collection to represent humans as they are. On the outside, on our covers, we may look clean and put together, but on the inside we have a story to tell. Our stories are both separate from each other and built on each other to create who we are. Our internal stories are not perfect, even if we display them as such. It is impossible to be perfect, but it is not impossible to be beautiful. That's what I wanted to display in my illustrations; messy, imperfect, and unfinished, but still beautiful and whole in the end.

I hope that as you read through this collection, that you find yourself with a feeling of familiarity and safety. I hope that it helps you know that you are never alone, even in your darkest of days. I hope that you find inspiration and hope because you are strong and deserve to press on. Remember that your dark days are merely a piece of you, they are not who you are. And if it feels like the whole world is alienating you, I hope this collection can be your home.

And I Close My Eyes

To Hide the Fear 1

To Recover From the Fight 33

To Dream of Hope 63

    Acknowledgements 93

    Final Thoughts 94

To Hide the Fear

There is a flutter in my bones,
Something thick
Something cold
Something that whispers
In the night
I fear it's poison
One more day
Just let me go
One more day, I plead
Leave me alone
But the voices still haunt me
They clog up my head
For the night
Is never truly dead

-A Fear of the Dark

To Hide the Fear

The wind blows north,
The sun heads west
The clouds flood in
The hope drowns out
The helplessness gets stronger
The days grow longer
The mind grows darker
The storm is coming
The light is fading

-The Rain is Beautiful Though

The night is scary
It's cold, it's dark
Some call it art

I call it fear
Fear swelling in my head
Until I'm dead
Fear so heavy
So lonely
That all I can do is run
Hoping for an escape
It's so painful to know
I'm alone in this cold
And this fear
Is all I have left
It consumes me

The night whispers
Sweet nothings fill the air
Some call it love

I call it terror
Terror because for all
I know
When I wake tomorrow
I'll still have silence
No one to talk to
No one to hug
I'll still be alone in this world
Maybe I always was

To Hide the Fear

The night's cold fingers
Caress my hips
Some call it passion

I call it death
Impending death
That never leaves my side
It tells me good morning
It kisses me good night
Gently touching my hand
To remind me
That at any moment
My world could come crashing down
And everything I had would be gone
All I'd have left is tears
Or maybe I'm next
Maybe it's me whose time is ticking
Maybe I'm not going to wake
And see tomorrow
Maybe the warning is for me

All the beautiful things
You see in the night
Are not who the night
Shows me
You're in love
And I'm abused
By the 'love' the night shows me

-Thinking in the Dark

Me?
I'm a package
I come with
Stretch marks
I come with scars
If you look closely
At my legs,
If you look closely
At my arms,
You'll see the remanence
Of the pain
Once ignored

Who could love
These stretch marks
Who could love
These scars
Who could love
Me
And us
For what we really are
Once you know my secrets
Once you hear my story
You'll forget
You ever loved me
But you never did
Anyway

-I Need to Accept Myself

To Hide the Fear

Your hands have never touched me
So why do I fear they have?
Your eyes have never traced me
But when asked, you come to mind
Your heart never came out of line
Yet I tremble when thoughts cross me
Am I imagining things?
Is this real?
Did I forget something
That I still feel?
Why can I hear it
But I cannot see it?
Why do you haunt me
With no story to prove it?
Leave me alone
I want my freedom
I want my hope

-The Line Between Truths and Lies

And I Close My Eyes

I feel like I'm drowning
With no water in sight
I feel like I'm suffocating
With plenty of air
I feel like I'm dead
And completely aware

-Perception Kills

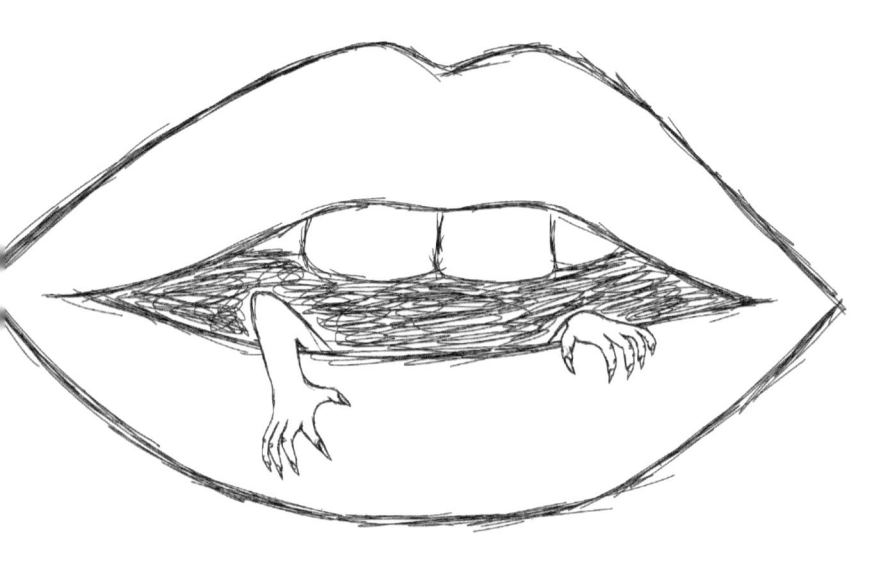

How can
Something I loathe
Something I hate
Hurt me so bad
When it's time to let go?

I will never accept you
I will never embrace you
But I'm helpless without you
And I already feel the break
That my heart will endure
Just knowing
That I wasted you away

So many times
I've avoided
And dreaded
And hated you here
But I know now that I'm leaving
And it hurts
I guess this feeling
This relationship with you
Is translated into my brain
Abusive, yes it's true

To Hide the Fear

I hold on to the feeling
That I denied I'd ever get
The love of being thrown around
Of being mistreated
And ignored
What will I do without it?
Can I succeed?
Instead of letting this relationship
This emotion
Control me?

-Self Destruction

There's an intensity in me
Like burning rage
It locks me inside
I scream with pain
I want to rip myself apart
Tearing until I'm free
But I just came back together
They say that I'm healing
But it's only a prison
There is only one escape
But I can't do that now
I'm petrified
For this pain keeps me here
This pain is me

-Sabotage

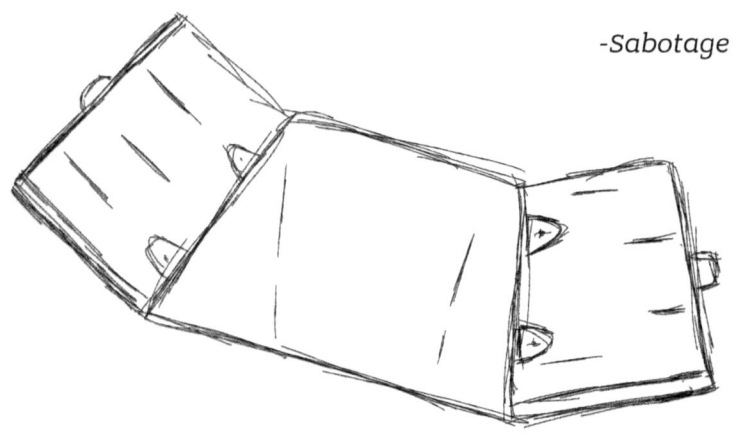

To Hide the Fear

When the night
Crawled closer
My dread
Grew bigger
I knew
That before long
You would show up
And sing your song
Do the dance
You thought I fell for
Say the words
You thought I believed
And take my heart
That you thought I gave you
But you see
When you're too young
To know the word
No
Consent
Isn't even a yes
I didn't say either one

But that was enough
For you
To poison me

-Reflections

There are times
In my life
Just for a blink of an eye
I feel so empty
I feel so cold
I feel completely distant,
So far that no one could
Hold me
When that was all I needed
For a split second
Just a momentary light
I see in the hallway
A masterpiece
That is me
A masterpiece that says
It's an original
But it's just a copy
I can pretend that
I'm different
I can pretend that
I've changed
But I'm only a replica
And that's how you made me

-It's Art

To Hide the Fear

You asked me to jump
I asked how high
You asked me to learn
I asked how much
You asked me to smile
I asked how big
You asked me to be quiet
I asked how long
You asked me to hate her
I couldn't do that
You asked what my use was
I smiled and shrugged
You forced me to hide
While you fed her lies
I couldn't even ask why

-To the Yearning Child

How is it
That the weight of
Your words
Was more
Than the weight of
Your hands

-The Words Last Longer

And I Close My Eyes

Biting cold
Pierces my skin
The places I have never been
They haunt my dreams
And kill my screams
And all I can do is freeze

She creeps in the night
Dangerously beautiful
As graceful as snow

Cunning and cold
She entices you
With her hair
She distracts you
With her eyes
But if you look too far inside
You see she has poison to hide
Soon you will too

Biting cold
Pierces my skin
The places I have never been
They haunt my dreams
And kill my screams
And all I can do is freeze

He walks in daylight
Sauntering in the sun
Sparkling in the light
His light blue eyes
Whisper trust
Don't look too close
He lies
He waits until you reach out
Run your fingers through his hair

To Hide the Fear

He waits until you trust him
Suddenly he's not there
Instead you see blind rage
Flying up in the air
Burning daylight
To ash
You're scared

Biting cold
Pierces my skin
The places I have never been
They haunt my dreams
And kill my screams
And all I can do is freeze

The last one is different
She's not who you know
She's bubbly and she's funny
You've seen her as so
But when the other two whisper
Her facade starts to blister
And suddenly she's the worst of all
She taunts and she daunts
And I cannot escape her
For she is me in the flesh

Biting cold
Pierces my skin
The places I have never been
They haunt my dreams
And kill my screams
And all I can do is freeze

-Who's the Real Enemy

And I Close My Eyes

The door was closed
You were far away
But I could still hear
Her scream

-The Sounds Carry

To Hide the Fear

When you look
At your Hands
Do you still
See my
Blood

-*Remembering Hurts*

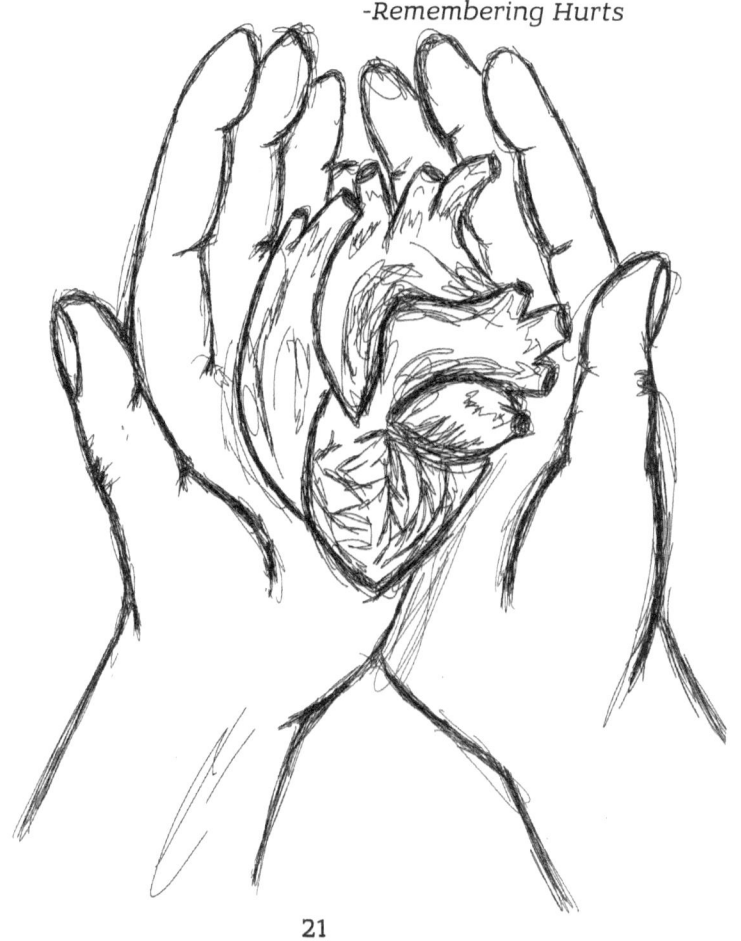

Glass
On all my sides
Shattered
Nowhere to hide
Walls
Trap me inside
Fear
The hope lied
Buried
By all I knew
Suffocated
By lies you told
Light
Drained from my eyes
Worlds
About to collide
Lives
Ready to end
Nothing
Will ever bend

-An Impossible Death

They looked at her in awe
Wishing they could be like her

She would rather
Be anyone else

-Open Your Eyes

I do not want to fall
Into this trap again
And yet
Here I am
Falling
Again
And

Again

-I'm Begging You to Save Me

To Hide the Fear

I said sorry
But I couldn't say why
I said it was my fault
But I couldn't say how
I said you should hate me
But I couldn't tell the story
I cry every night
But I won't tell a soul
I wish for forgiveness
But how can you forgive what you don't know?
I want to smile once more
But the memories haunt me
I hear the thoughts stalking me
But none of it is real
I asked for your love
But I don't even love me

-I'm My Own Enemy

Even when you
Love me
You never
Truly do

-Say it to My Face

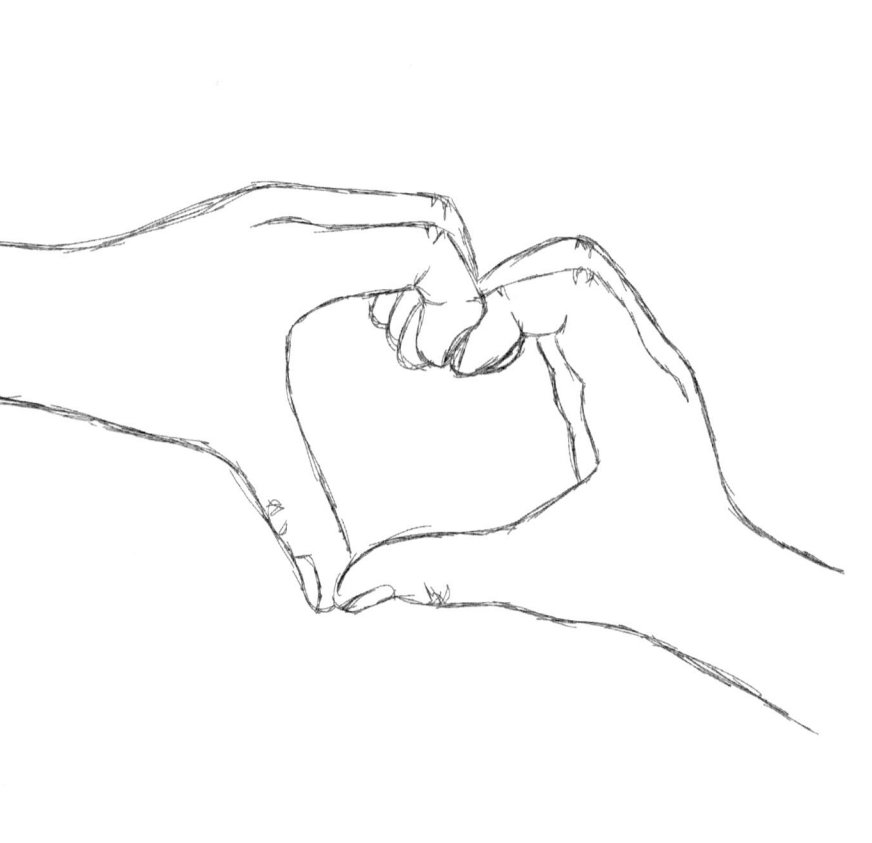

Sometimes I wonder
If you even know
How sick you are

-Questions I Shouldn't Ask

To Hide the Fear

Pretty people
Passing by
Pretty people
I wonder why
Pretty people
Choose to lie
Making other
Pretty people
Cry

-Pain is Not a Hobby

My thoughts race
Something sour
Something vile
A haunting image
A picture of nothing
That whispers distress
What would happen
If when I next slept
I never woke?

Would she know
How she made me smile?
Would she know
How I loved her company?
Would she know
That I admired her
With every bone in my body?

Would he know
That he only made me stronger
With every moment
That his fear
Was injected into my veins?

Would he know
That I'd take a bullet
Before I'd let those words hurt him?
Would he know
All the pain I felt
When he turned his cheek?

To Hide the Fear

Would she know
I savored her touch
Her smile
And her laugh?

I couldn't live without them in my life
Who would they see
If I never woke up
If I could never be
Who I wanted to be
And they couldn't see
What I saw of them in me

-Tell Me You Know

To Recover From the Fight

There is a darkness
There is a terror
Hidden up in that tower
I fear the death
And depression
They keep locked up
But curiosity strikes my nose

Again
And I creep to the lock
With a thought
Of how the door knob stings
The whispers cry
And my ears, they ring
A thought
Of this lock

And how it's here
For a reason
And I'm messing
With power
With which I cannot reason
A thought
Of the regret I'll feel
When I know
What's behind this door
I should go
Just go
Maybe I need saving
Maybe I need grace
But whatever's behind that door

To Recover From the Fight

Is only a mistake
So I'll wait

I'll wait

-It Beckons Me

The tears
They scream
They kiss
They burn
But
Through the pain
I smile at you

-I Don't Want You to See

To Recover From the Fight

And I close my eyes
So I may be free of reality
For just a drunk moment
With a smile
So delicately close
I picture us
In a life far from this cold
Away from this terror
Not running from our fears
Not crying lonesome tears
Far from this reality
Just happy
Just smiling
So save me some silence
When my eyes are closed
For I am escaping
From this sober reality

-Can You See the Freedom?

I can never tell
If this is just a game

Or something more

-Do Your Lips Speak the Truth?

To Recover From the Fight

If I am a flower
When will I bloom?
If I am a star
When will I shine?
If I am a kid
When will I play?
If I am a woman
Where is my strength?
If I am of her
Where is my thin figure?
If I am of him
Where's my fire?
If I am only human
When will I live?
If I am alive
When will I smile?
If I have potential
Why can't I find it?
If you loved me
Why did you do it?

-Pointless Wishes

I
Will
Not
Be
Controlled
By
The
Thought
Of
You

-And I Mean it

To Recover From the Fight

I never knew
That even the way
That I took my breaths
Were changed
By you

I wasn't *taking* them
I was asking for them

I'm done asking

I deserve to breathe.

-Self Worth Tastes Sweet

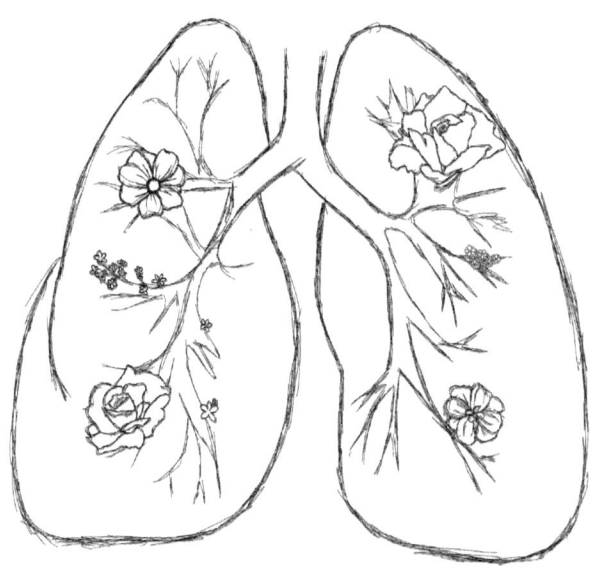

And I Close My Eyes

Although I would love
To meet you
I worry
About what you'll see
Inside of me

-I'm Afraid of Me

To Recover From the Fight

You spark
A war in me
Between
What I thought
I knew
And all I now know
From you

-A War for the Better

And I Close My Eyes

I think I forgot
How to put my foot down

If you can use yours
To walk all over me

I can use mine
To tell you

No.

-Don't Mess With My Boundaries

To Recover From the Fight

She was alone in the world
But only in her heart
She was strong and she was beautiful
But she was blind
She was resilient
But you continued to beat her
She was bruised and she was broken
But she kept fighting anyway
She was drowning in the waves
But she held her breath
She smiled at the world
But she feared them
She was kind to everyone
But she hid her imperfections
She had dreams and she had goals
But she spent so long searching for them
She had given up hope
But she told herself to keep going
She was out of breath and she was hurt
But she didn't think
She had the right to cry

-Strength Bites Back

I am not a flower
So why did you pick me?
I am not glass
So why did you shatter me?
I am not yours
So why did you control me?
I am not yours
So I will take back
My life
I am not glass
So I will rebuild
What you broke
I am not a flower
So I will not die
I will grow stronger

-I Am Not of Your Making

To Recover From the Fight

Maybe I am all that
You say I am

But I'm tired of this
Letting it control my life
Over and
Over
Does it ever end?

I can't fight back
Surrender is my only choice

Except
It's not

You might never
Ever stop
Over using me
Upsetting me
Recurring in my mind

How could you
After all
Nothing you ever
Did was
Small

-So I Will Fight to Survive

And I Close My Eyes

I hear you
Inhaling life
And exhaling peace
I hear you
Taking gentle breaths
Your eyes softly closed
Your soul at ease
As you sleep
I hear you
And the life you hold
As you lay next to me
So why do I feel so alone
So empty and cold
So numb and distraught
Like my brain is reaching out
Desperate for a hand to hold
How is it possible
To feel so lonely
When I'm not
Alone

-Do You Hear Me Too?

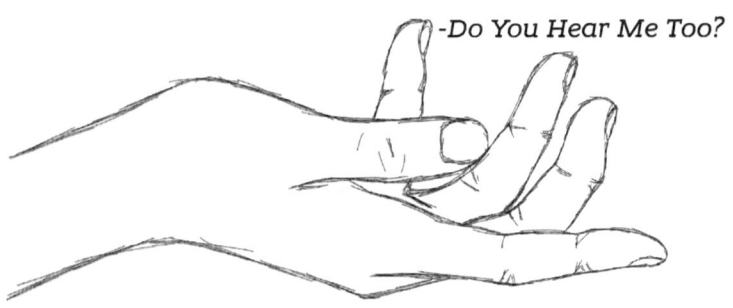

To Recover From the Fight

Even when she smiles
She fights like a warrior
Holding her head high
She battles her demons
Day and night
She never gets
To stop and breathe
Because even when she smiles
She's in pain

-The Never Ending War

Am I blaming
Everything on you
Even if it's not
Your fault
Or
Am I not allowing
Myself to be
Broken
By what would break
Anyone

-Fragile or Weak?

To Recover From the Fight

Why do I cling
To something
So damn
Poisonous
That it burns
Through my veins
With every sip
I guess
That's what they call
Addiction

-Can't Get Enough

Help
She whispered
Making sure no one
Could hear

-The Silent Cry

To Recover From the Fight

The world is dark
It's dreary
Sometimes it scratches
At my skin
Sometimes I bleed
Sometimes I can't breathe
But
I can't cry
No
I can't cry
Who can I tell
Can I tell you?
No
I can't tell you
You'd think me weak
But paper
Paper can't watch me break
Paper can't judge me
When I'm at the the brink

-My Safety Lies Here

Be quiet
You said
Be quiet
They demanded
Be quiet
You yelled
Be quiet
They pleaded
But now
Now is not the time
To be quiet
Now is a time
To be loud
To roar
And to yell
To whisper
And to scream
Because for all the times
You told me be quiet
Now I must
Yell

Don't tell me
To be quiet

-Silence is a Trap

To Recover From the Fight

The war
Between the want
To hurt
And
To be helped
Will kill me

-So What Do I Do?

Sunflower
How are you
So bright
And beautiful
Even when
You fight
Your whole life
Just to stay alive

-Beauty

To Recover From the Fight

I wish I could
Rewind
I wish I could
Pause
I wish I could
Stop
The pain from
Haunting
You

-But I'm Powerless

I can't keep the touch
Away from my head
I want a break
From what I've seen
What I've felt
What was said

The sting
Of your touch
Is only the start
It spirals
Into a beating wave
Of painful memories

Some of them
Don't even belong to me
But then again
Not even you
Belong
In my head

-The Connections Are Even Worse

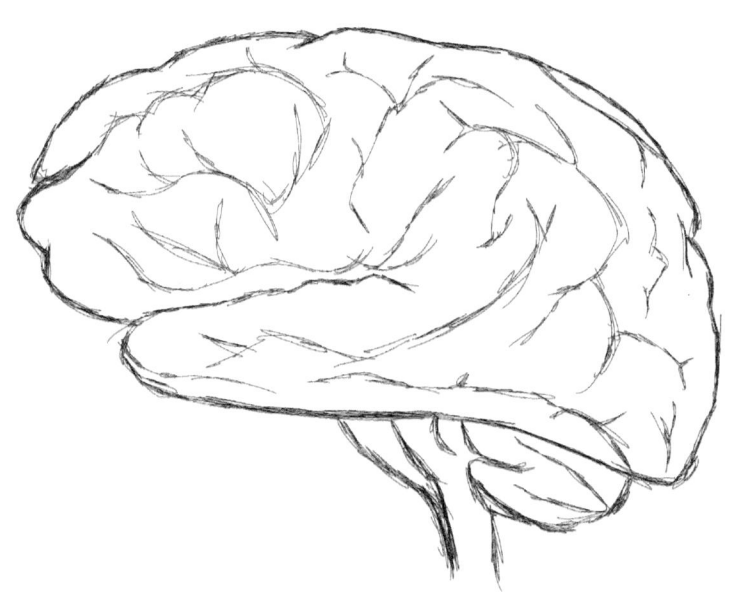

Always this time
Always the winter
Always this season
The seasons trigger
The memories that live
In the ice
So this winter
Keep your hands off me
Keep your touch
Away from my heart
Keep those memories
To yourself

This winter
I want to be happy

-When It's Cold, I Think

To Recover From the Fight

I am a delicacy
Golden on your tongue
But when you take me
For granted
I'll be sure
That I'm laced with
Poison
Next time you take
What was never truly
Yours

-Don't Overstay Your Welcome

To Dream of Hope

To Dream of Hope

The wind blows faster
The lives fly past her
Her hopes for others never fading
Just one look at the light she's creating
I could not explain her more
Than the calm in the middle of a storm

Her eyes hold such peace
Her mind at such ease
Her hair flowing gold
All the strength in a best friend's hold
That's not all, she's so much more
Than the calm in the middle of a storm

Without her I'd be no more
Her soul no less than a roar
She's graceful
She's peaceful
She means so much more to me
Than the calm in the middle of a storm

-She's Home

Hush
My baby
Don't you cry
I want you to smile
Notice how life
Goes by

Hush
My baby
Don't you fret
You're only human
Perfection doesn't exist

Hush
My baby
Things always get better
Don't beat yourself up
You're always beautiful
To me

Hush
My baby
I want you to be happy
I want you to smile
Don't hurt yourself
Because you think
You've failed me

To Dream of Hope

Hush
My baby
I love you no matter what
You should try to love you too

-You Deserve Love

I know you're hurt
I know you're scared
In this cruel world
You can never be prepared

I know you're tired
I know you're crying
You're in pain
Just know I'm trying

I know you're fearful
I know you're helpless
That look in your eyes
Makes me scared and breathless

I know you can make it
I know you can try
So I leave you with hope
So I say goodbye

-There is Happiness to be Found

Skies of blue
Seas of green
and all the weight
That can be carried
In a dream
I wish for you
Every night
I pray for you
In broad daylight
To change your ways
To make things straight
Not for me
But for her
So I can see her smile
Forevermore

-But I'm Powerless to Fate

To Dream of Hope

I sink into your ocean
More and more
Everyday
I take in
Every moment
Like a breath
But
I will not drown

-You Give Me Life

And I Close My Eyes

I'm intoxicated
By your touch
Every time you caress my cheek
I blush
I breathe you in and out again
Getting high off every breath
Your scent fills me with a calm
That I've never found elsewhere
And I fall into a heaven
I slip into a trance
When the petals from your flowers
Chose to show me a dance
Every move is swift
Every second is fluid
I rest my hands on your hips
And you teach me how to dance
We sway with the wind
We flow with the sun
We race with the water
We dance
We sing
We love

To Dream of Hope

There's something in my heart
I only feel with you
When I dance with this flower
It all comes through
So stay with me
For one more song
So I can just
Dance with you

-So This is Love

And I Close My Eyes

Do you know
How much
Your company means
To me

-Sit With Me if You Feel the Same

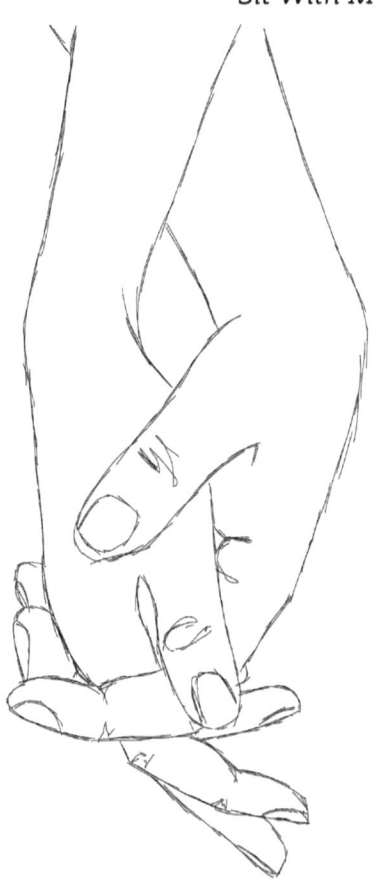

To Dream of Hope

I thought that
I had moved on
But I heard your voice
And realized that
I never left

-I Think I Belong Here

And I Close My Eyes

I wish that I could paint the sky
With every whisper
Every cry
Every moment ever wasted
Carefully, thoughtfully pasted
Forever trapped in a time
Peaceful, with no crime
I wish that I could paint the sky
So that this feeling
Will never die
Every smile ever fading
The future is kept waiting
Every set of eyes that flutter closed
A bit of hope being imposed
I wish that I could paint the sky
So that I wouldn't have to miss you
And this wouldn't be goodbye

-I Wish to See Happiness

To Dream of Hope

When I feel
Like I can't go on
Will you take my hand
And pull me forward

-Isn't Trust a Burden?

And I Close My Eyes

I am mesmerized
By every word
That falls off your tongue

I am entranced
By your voice
It seems to wrap
Around my body
And pull me
Into the safest hug

I'm forever longing
To hear you laugh
Again
Because it never fails
To make me smile

As your eyes
Light up
And I fall into
A trance
For once
Just for a moment
All I feel in my soul
Is you
And the happiness
You give me

To Dream of Hope

Your infectious
Beauty
Washes over me
Like a huge wave
It encompasses my entire body
At once
And then
When it's over
I still feel
The remnants
Of your
Smile
In my
Heart

-The Ocean

Feet
Walking without a care
Hands
Gliding here and there
Stop
Judging me, I don't care
Words
Mean nothing when you're there
Smile
Give me one that's real
Happiness
Ecstasy in the air
Nothing
In this world mattered to me
Nothing truly matters unless
That nothing
Is you

-Concepts

To Dream of Hope

The darkness held her
So tight
For so long
That she forgot
What it was like
To be kissed
By the sun

-Can I Ask for Redemption?

I know
That you've heard it before
I know
That it's cliché
But when a flower grows
In the cracks of the pavement

It gives me hope
That one day
You'll be able
To grow through
The cracks of my heart
And blossom into something
Beautiful
Something
Wonderful
Something called
Trust
Something called
Love

-A Tale as Old as Concrete

To Dream of Hope

If I told you that
You were my only
Solace
Would you stay with me
A little longer

-Probably a Delusion

The burn
Of your hands
Lingered
On my arms
Until I replaced it
With the healing touch
Of love

The hiss
Of your words
Echoed
In my ears
Until I erased it
With the soothing melodies
Of love

The horrors
You showed me
Replayed
In my mind
Until I rewrote it
With the pure beauty
Of love

To Dream of Hope

You hurt me
In every way possible
But
Love will always
Heal pain
And I
Found someone
Who loves me
In every way possible

-Some Powers are Greater

Progress
Is not
A forward march
It has no rhythm
It has no direction
It is a drunken stumble
A beautiful dance
Forward
Backward
Right
And left
It is unpredictable
It is scary
It is filled with trips
It is scattered with falls
It involves bruises
And scrapes
But
It is healing

Though progress
Feels daunting
And impossible at times
Remember
It is never a straight line
The road
Of healing
Is made of rough terrain
You will stumble
You must get up again

To Dream of Hope

I promise
The beauty
When you reach
The top
When you see
The fields
And the pain
Finally stops
Will be worth
Every time
You almost gave up
Or you almost stopped
All of your fighting
Your resilience
And your strength

Here you can breathe
And find yourself again

-The Road to Happiness

There's a song in my mind
A rhythm I can't defy
The words whisper wisdom
And the beat yells emotion
I stomp my feet
I wave my arms
Yet the roar never calms
So I write

Every word caresses my skin
Every letter nibbles my ear
I'm in love with this feeling
So I let it win
The butterflies in my stomach
Tell my mind what to do
As I write out a poem
Gentle yet true

Soon they get restless
They just can't let it out
They start to scream
They start to shout
I'm no longer in love
with the words on this page
They sting my skin
They're born with rage
I scribble
And scribble
As fast as I can

To Dream of Hope

But the words don't leave fast enough
They never can
Tears run down my cheeks
They scream louder
I scream back
I've never felt a pain
Like this
Take it back
Take it back

Nibbles turn to bites
There's blood running down my skin
Reopened wounds
In places that have never been
I cry
I try to run
But I can never escape
The music
That trickles through my veins

Suddenly its over
All I can say is on a page
And the drumming in my heart
Quiets
And becomes a soft
Thump
Thump
Thump
Of safety

Quiet washes over me
The agony is all gone
And I realize that the pain
Was love
All along
Supporting me
Through this song
The wounds may be hidden
But they were there all along
Sometimes we must hurt
To discover what's wrong

My words are now on a page
Beautiful and strong
For now it's all over
But soon I'll start again
When the drumming in my head
Says that there's more
To be said

Now read my song
And feel my pain
And I'll see you later
When the music
Is back again

-There's More to be Said

Acknowledgements

Working on this poetry collection was scary, daunting, and thrilling. The courage and confidence I needed to create and publish this would not have been possible without Galli Huaute for her editing and advice, as well as Natalia Junqueira for her cover design and typesetting. Galli and my boyfriend, Torrin Martel, were so important in supporting, encouraging, and helping me throughout this whole process. I would also like to thank those who have supported me up to this point: my family and friends for their support, my past teachers who encouraged me and guided me into the strength I have today, and everyone else along the way who made me who I am. I hold you all close to my heart and I could never thank you enough for what you've done for me.

Final Thoughts

Writing this collection was not something I had originally done for the purpose of publishing. These poems were my way of working through emotions and understanding the things that I thought and felt when it seemed like emotions were out of my reach. I had such a hard time both deciphering what I was facing and putting that into comprehensible sentences, but when I really needed a bridge between the deep turmoil inside and the tangible world, poetry was there for me. It was the one thing that I could lean on when I just needed a way to connect with myself.

I think that it's very important to note that this collection is structured in an uphill slope intentionally. When I wrote the poems, they did not follow the straight forward progression that this collection does because I was healing, and healing is not a straight line. There were times when I wrote about hope and acceptance, but then the following day I would write about being hopeless, lost, and empty. That is what healing encompasses. We stumble backwards, we leap forward, and sometimes we go nowhere at all. It is so important that we all accept that about ourselves, as hard as that is, because progress is progress, even when it feels as though we are moving backwards.

Deciding to finally publish this collection was a decision I made because I know the impact that poetry has on people. Not only that, but it was a test of my own personal acceptance. It was extremely difficult to put these words onto paper that the whole world could see, as every word here was so incredibly personal that putting it out into the world was a terrifying thought. Maybe reading my words will be the connection someone out there needs in order to feel less alone, or maybe I'll inspire others to find an outlet through writing their own poetry. My words should not only be for me; there are so many people in the world who are facing their own adversities, need hope, need to hear words that they connect to, and that need to find encouragement to move forward. Those people may find what they need in my writing. All of the internal battles that I fought will have been worth it if my words can help ease the pain that others face. I made it through my struggles by falling into books and poetry, and I know how much that connection is worth. I made this because I know how precious that brief moment is when you feel as though someone has been through something that you are facing, knowing that they made it out alive, that they are stronger than ever, and that you can do it too. I hope that I can provide that feeling, as well as that strength to someone who needs it.

That is why I chose to publish this collection.

Together, we are stronger than we could ever be alone. Allow me to walk with you on your journey, and to give you all the strength I can to keep moving forward.

www.ingramcontent.com/pod-product-compliance
Lightning Source LLC
Chambersburg PA
CBHW020912080526
44589CB00011B/561